I0422823

The Unshakable Confidence

Strategies to Build Unstoppable Confidence in Order to Achieve Goals and Live a Fulfilling Life

By

Ruben B. Campbell

Copyright © **2024** by ***Ruben B. Campbell***.
ISBN: 9798884733305. All rights reserved. This
book or any piece thereof may not be replicated
or utilized by any stretch of the imagination
using any means without the consent of the
Writer/distributer except for the use of brief
references in a book survey.

Disclaimer

The information provided in this book, "*The Unshakeable Confidence: Strategies to Build Unstoppable Confidence in Order to Achieve Goals and Live a Fulfilling Life,*" is for educational and informational purposes only. The author and publisher of this book are not licensed professionals, and the content provided should not be considered a substitute for professional advice, diagnosis, or treatment.

The strategies and techniques outlined in this book are based on the author's personal experiences, research, and observations. While every effort has been made to ensure the accuracy and completeness of the information provided, the author and publisher make no guarantees regarding the results that may be achieved by implementing these strategies.

It is important to consult with qualified professionals, such as licensed therapists, counselors, or coaches, before making any significant changes to your life or implementing the techniques discussed in this book. Each individual's circumstances are unique, and what works for one person may not work for another.

The author and publisher disclaim any liability for any loss or damage resulting from reliance on the information provided in this book. The reader assumes full responsibility for their actions and decisions based on the content of this book.

By reading this book, the reader agrees to release the author and publisher from any and all liability arising from the use or misuse of the information provided herein. The reader also acknowledges that their success or failure in implementing the strategies outlined in this book is dependent on their own efforts, abilities, and circumstances.

Please use your discretion and judgment when applying the techniques and strategies discussed in this book. Your well-being and success are important, and it is recommended to seek professional guidance when needed.

About the Author

Ruben B. Campbell is a passionate writer dedicated to the field of personal development. With a deep-rooted belief in the transformative power of self-improvement, Ruben has dedicated his career to helping others unlock their full potential and live their best lives.

Drawing on his own personal experiences and extensive research in the field of psychology, self-help, and personal growth, Ruben has authored numerous books aimed at guiding readers on their journey towards personal and professional success.

With a clear and engaging writing style, Ruben's books offer practical strategies, actionable advice, and insightful perspectives on topics ranging from confidence-building and goal-setting to mindset mastery and resilience.

Ruben's commitment to empowering others extends beyond his writing, as he actively engages with his audience through workshops, seminars, and online communities. His passion for personal development is infectious, inspiring readers to take charge of their lives, pursue their passions, and create meaningful change.

Whether you're looking to boost your confidence, overcome self-doubt, or achieve your goals, Ruben's books provide the guidance and inspiration you need to embark on your own journey of personal growth and transformation. With Ruben as your guide, the possibilities for self-improvement are limitless.

Table of Contents

Introduction

Let me tell you this, Maybe what prevents any solution to fix yourself is the realization that you were never broken in the first place. you were born naturally confident.

Despite your current beliefs, confidence is your innate, default condition. Contrary to common perception, achieving confidence, embracing self-worth, and effortlessly attaining your goals isn't arduous. It's merely a matter of executing the correct steps in the proper sequence. it's a steps

The issue lies in the fact that much of the instruction on confidence is inverted. Essentially, all you require is to understand one straightforward yet crucial principle to cultivate the innate, unshakeable confidence characteristic of the top 1% who reach their aspirations, excel in their endeavors, and dictate their own terms in life. Once you internalize this fundamental principle, nothing can impede your advancement.

This is it:

"You're not flawed, and there's no need for repairs. You possess all the elements necessary for confidence and to craft the precise life you desire. It's a matter of shedding the detrimental programming and erroneous beliefs you've acquired, unlocking the immense potential within you."

Pause and reflect on this. When a baby is born, it doesn't doubt its worthiness of love, care, or attention. Similarly, a young child taking its first steps or learning a language doesn't believe it's incapable of achieving those milestones. When encountering new faces, a baby doesn't harbor feelings of inadequacy or inferiority compared to others. These notions aren't inherent; they're acquired through learning.

Understanding this reality, you recognize that any feeling of inadequacy regarding your identity and potential is unnatural and stems from misguided teachings. It becomes evident that any lack of confidence doesn't reflect your intrinsic worth but rather the influence of external instruction. The unconscious misconception shared by many is that guidance from parents, teachers, and peers is geared towards facilitating our success - that what we're taught is essential for thriving in life.

However, what if this assumption isn't accurate?

If that were the case, then surely more than 1% of individuals would be living the lives they genuinely desire, rather than settling for lives filled with frustration and quiet desperation. So, perhaps the most surprising and exhilarating proposition I want to present to you is this: You have always been, and you always will be, completely in charge of your confidence and the outcomes in your life.

When I convey this idea to people, they often object and list all the "reasons" why they feel the way they do and why they believe they can't attain the life they desire: lack of finances, not possessing the same level of attractiveness as others, absence of the ideal job or connections, time constraints, and countless others. Naturally, they are correct, aren't they?

NO
Regardless of your current life situation or personal circumstances, I will demonstrate how

you can rapidly enhance both your self-esteem and your life outcomes. By rediscovering your core essence, shedding unproductive thoughts and negative programming, and embracing the innate success mindset utilized by the top 1% achievers, you'll find that success in life becomes foreseeable and unavoidable.

The purpose of writing this book is to equip you with precise tools, techniques, and strategies, presenting a detailed step-by-step process. These resources will empower you to cultivate unshakable, unstoppable self-confidence and a mindset that propels your life results from ordinary to extraordinary success. You'll transition from a life marked by missed opportunities and unrealized potential to one of remarkable and assured success. No longer at the mercy of circumstances, you'll boldly step forward, making a significant impact on the world.

Your dent on the universe.

If that resonates with you, then you're in for a treat with what this book has to offer. However, there are a couple of crucial points to address.

Firstly, many of the concepts, methods, and strategies presented in this book diverge from conventional teachings and wisdom. You won't encounter these techniques in the majority of self-help literature or from most therapists.

I urge you to approach this with an open mind. As you delve into the contents of this book, I encourage you to refrain from passing judgment and instead, simply contemplate the ideas presented.

Your existing mindset has shaped your current reality. Embracing different perspectives will lead you toward the life you desire. This book contains such perspectives, although they may challenge or contradict what you currently perceive as true.

Your ego, the negative inner voice, will likely attempt to immediately discredit these new concepts. It may assert that you "already know this," or that "everybody knows [insert common thought here] is true." When these moments arise, take a moment to pause and carefully consider the information. You can always judge and dismiss later, but for now, allow yourself to explore what is being presented.

Moreover, your ego may frequently suggest that while others could achieve the results discussed, you cannot. This is a deceitful tactic your mind employs to keep you stagnant. Refrain from falling for this falsehood. Instead, recognize the truth: you are not so uniquely incapable that this methodology works for everyone else but you.

You deserve the opportunity to shape the life you desire. Permit yourself to contemplate the genuine possibilities for your future. You've likely spent numerous years fixated on what you perceive as impossible. Therefore, take a temporary reprieve from that mindset. You can always revert to it later if needed.

Next, you'll observe a deliberate repetition throughout the book. This repetition serves a specific purpose.

My primary goal is for you to unlock the innate confidence and success within you, enabling you to attain the life you truly desire.

Unlike many other books that convey information only once, presuming that reading it equates to understanding, I intentionally repeat key points. This approach is crucial, as it counters one of the main reasons why numerous self-help books fall short in generating lasting transformation.

A well-known adage suggests that "Our habits define us. Excellence, therefore, is not an isolated action but a consistent habit."

For you, this implies that merely perusing this content won't lead to the desired outcomes.

Achieving the results you seek involves not just reading, but also pondering the concepts presented, and most crucially, implementing the techniques and strategies.

Consistently applying them is key.

This is the blueprint for human learning and mastering any skill. It's ineffective unless you engage in all the components. Partial efforts won't suffice, much like constructing only parts of a house won't yield a functional dwelling.

As you encounter repetition in the book, view it as a cue to assess your understanding and, more significantly, to evaluate whether you've truly applied and mastered a concept—or if you merely believe you have.

There's a significant difference

Every constraint in our lives stems from the misconceptions we've permitted in our minds. Through persistent examination, these falsehoods gradually dissolve, revealing their illusory nature.

Once identified, you eliminate the hidden barriers impeding your path to realizing your dreams.

So, are you prepared for a change?

Let's proceed directly to cultivating Unwavering Confidence within You.

Chapter 1

Awakening Your Inborn Success Mindset

Do you have the courage to challenge your perception of yourself.?

What if I were to say that you're perfectly fine as you are? That you're whole and don't require any repairs?

In fact, it's quite the opposite—your inherent nature is one of confidence and success. The only obstacle is the set of detrimental and constraining beliefs that have been instilled in you through teachings, conditioning, and societal influences, hindering your innate success mindset and confidence.

The lack of improvement you've experienced is due to approaching the core issue in reverse. You don't require additional information, programming, or conditioning added to your mind.

You need to do precisely the Opposite

Instead, you must shed all the restrictive and harmful thinking patterns that inhibit your natural confidence and success mindset from functioning as intended.

Most conventional personal development approaches advocate for changing oneself to feel good and achieve confidence and success. Not only is this approach incorrect, but it's also profoundly detrimental. Let's examine this more closely to understand why.

The underlying premise of such teachings is that one must transform into someone different in order to improve, succeed, be accepted, and loved. For someone already struggling with feelings of inadequacy, this reinforces their belief that they are inherently unworthy.

Now, you find yourself feeling even worse than before, sensing even greater distance from your dreams. You start to perceive yourself as somehow flawed, unlike the confident and successful individuals you admire.

In an attempt to improve, you dive into more books, enroll in additional courses, and push yourself harder. Yet, each resource seems to highlight more aspects of yourself that you lack and need to change. This only serves to reinforce your sense of inadequacy and distance from your desired state.

Your efforts to help yourself begin to backfire, as each new piece of information pushes you further away from your goals. Instead of feeling better and more confident, you feel increasingly worse with each revelation.

Indeed, there's a need to deviate from the persona you've adopted, but it's not about changing away from your true self. Rather, it's about reverting back to who you really are.

Returning to Inborn Confidence

Allow me to elaborate

Embedded deeply within your genetic makeup from the moment of conception and coursing through every cell in your body is a remarkable, resilient blueprint for achieving virtually any conceivable goal.

This blueprint was installed onto the most remarkable and advanced supercomputer ever known: the human brain. This extraordinary machine can process immense quantities of data and execute a multitude of intricate tasks, even when dealing with incomplete or inaccurate information. Despite these challenges, it possesses the capability to arrive at precisely the correct solution.

The human mind - **your mind** - is a miracle.

Your fundamental, underlying programming is extraordinary.

Consider a newborn baby: Do they harbor any notion of unworthiness? Do they believe they shouldn't obtain what they desire? Are they hindered by thoughts that they can't achieve or become something?

These limitations are acquired; they don't align with your innate mindset. Those who exude natural confidence and success aren't inherently different from others. They simply, intentionally or inadvertently, haven't adopted the backward, convoluted thinking that impedes 99% of individuals.

Recognizing this, and more significantly, embodying it, transforms everything. Instead of believing you must transform into someone you're not, you realize that all you need to do is reconnect with your authentic self.

It's a markedly distinct journey, one that feels intuitive and effortless rather than challenging and arduous. This subtle shift creates a profound impact.

The 1% simply refused to accept failure. They recognized that the prescribed rules were ineffective and nonsensical.

The Flawed Framework

In addition to the detrimental programming regarding not measuring up in terms of worth, talent, or appearance, there are layers upon layers of expectations and limitations dictating who you "ought" to be, what you "should" desire, and the type of life you "should" pursue.

Now, your innate talents and confidence have been dulled, and you're propelled toward a notion of "success" that isn't truly your own—where even if you attain it, you've ultimately failed because it doesn't align with the life you consciously desired. It's a life dictated by others, not by your own choices.

Reflect on this: Are you living life on your own terms, or someone else's?

Take a moment to contemplate this. Don't rush to respond. There's immense value in grasping this concept.

Ask yourself candidly: Is the life you're presently leading the one you genuinely desire, one that you've intentionally and consciously crafted? Or did it simply unfold without much thought?

Despite what you might believe, no one's life simply unfolds by chance. You've fashioned the life you're living today, just like everyone else has. The challenge lies in the lack of conscious awareness regarding the blueprint you've been following—the one handed down by your parents, teachers, and peers.

And due to this lack of awareness, you likely didn't pause to assess whether it was the suitable path for you.

Have you ever pondered the origins of your worldview? This comprises the unique blueprint guiding your life: your fundamental beliefs, values, and the self-imposed rules dictating your existence.

Have you devoted any time to discerning your genuine desires in life?

- *The type of individual you aspired to be.*
- *The type of companion you envisioned having.*
- *What your life purpose was*
- *What your real dreams and ambitions were*

For 99% of individuals, the response to that query is a resounding NO! They aren't truly pursuing their desires; instead, they are pursuing what they have been CONDITIONED to desire. They crave what their parents instructed them to desire.

- *They want what their partners say they should want.*

- They want what their friends think "everyone should want

- They want what their teachers taught them they should want.

- They want what society expects them to want.

As a young child, you possessed a clear sense of your desires, unaffected by the opinions of others. Conforming to someone else's standards was inconceivable. Life held endless possibilities, and you knew you could achieve, experience, or acquire anything.

However, as you matured, societal influences gradually shaped your behavior. You were instructed on what to do, what to say, and what to think. Society's norms, the prescribed path to societal success, and the definition of a fulfilling life as dictated by others became ingrained.

Your true desires, what truly brought you joy, became obscured beneath layers of false programming and restrictive societal conditioning about how things should be.

Most significantly, you discovered the necessity of adhering to these rules and societal norms to gain acceptance and affection.

Your perception of the world, your interpretation of how things should unfold, is heavily influenced by the childhood recognition that love is contingent upon conformity. Consequently, we formulate a set of guidelines to fulfill these conditions and receive love.

The Two Vital Inquiries Shaping Almost Everyone's Existence

What influences could be potent enough to compel us to abandon or even disregard our true desires and comply with the wishes of others?

there are two questions that profoundly shape the lives of almost everyone. These questions reside at the very core of our psyche and ultimately influence our thoughts, choices, decisions, and actions.

These inquiries were:

1) Do I measure up?

2) Am I worthy of love?

At the deepest level, each of us is propelled by either one or both of these questions.

Our most profound apprehension, frequently concealed, is the belief that we are somehow inadequate or inherently undeserving of love.

The desires to feel "enough" and to be loved are fundamental, nearly instinctual requirements. Accomplishing these goals can prompt you to prioritize them above all else, whether consciously or subconsciously. You may even engage in self-destructive behaviors unconsciously to fulfill these needs.

In childhood, when your survival hinges on others, these fears can intensify significantly. Consequently, when approval, praise, or love is bestowed as a reward for adhering to societal expectations or withheld as a form of punishment for deviating from them, you may comply to the point of harming yourself.

Repeat this cycle frequently enough, and you'll lose sight of any alternative. Gradually, it becomes your new default mode of operation.

Instead of focusing on your genuine desires, you prioritize actions that validate your sense of worthiness or lovability according to arbitrary standards set by others.

In order to garner acceptance and affection, you begin to contort your own beliefs and principles to conform to these standards. With time, you become increasingly disconnected from your authentic desires and more aligned with the external blueprint.

Eventually, you find yourself completely misaligned, feeling utterly disoriented and disconnected from yourself. Like most individuals in this situation, you're likely bewildered by the sense of life's incomprehensibility and your own emotional turmoil.

How can you experience contentment when you're adhering to someone else's blueprint for your existence? When you've relinquished your genuine aspirations, passions, goals, and values?

When you've abandoned your authentic self?

You feel disheartened because you're exerting considerable effort to pursue a dream that isn't truly yours. You're tirelessly striving to inhabit a life that contradicts your genuine values and identity.

You're endeavoring to embody a persona that diverges from your authentic passions, identity, values, and purpose.

Conflict within oneself is inevitable, yet the most significant issue lies in the fact that few are even conscious of it.

How can life feel coherent when fulfilling fundamental needs necessitates acting contrary to your desires, dreams, and aspirations? How can you attain happiness, confidence, and success when you're at odds with your authentic desires?

If you aspire to lead a life that feels meaningful, the initial stride you must undertake is to break free from a blueprint that wasn't of your own making.

The primary step on this journey (which you've just embarked upon) is to recognize that you've been adhering to someone else's blueprint, someone else's vision for your life, and that you've lost sight of your genuine desires.

There is immense power in impartially observing how your thoughts, actions, and decisions conform to a model you didn't consciously select. Through this observation, you begin to discern the origins of the problems, pain, confusion, and unsuccessful choices in your life.

Grasping Your True Identity

The next pivotal step towards genuine and enduring transformation, towards embodying the person you genuinely aspire to be and crafting the life you authentically desire, involves reshaping your identity, your perception of self.

The primary reason why numerous individuals struggle to effect lasting change in their lives is that most approaches to personal development address the issue at the wrong depth.

It concentrates on altering your actions, yet it fails to transform your core identity.

The issue? This contradicts the innate functioning of our minds. Our self-perception fundamentally shapes every aspect of who we are and how we interact with the world. Our speech patterns, body language, eye contact, expression of thoughts and emotions, assertiveness, and confidence all originate from our self-image.

When you perceive yourself as worthy and deserving, when you take pride in who you are and feel confident in your place in the world, your behaviors, choices, and body language effortlessly reflect this. It feels natural, harmonious, and requires no conscious effort to maintain. You simply operate at that level as a matter of course.

However, if you perceive yourself as unworthy and undeserving, you can acquire knowledge about body language, eye contact, assertiveness, and other skills, and you may be able to implement each component individually. Nevertheless, these elements won't seamlessly integrate. Achieving alignment will require substantial effort, resulting in exhaustion, and ultimately, a regression to your previous default state. However, you won't simply revert to your previous state; you'll likely experience even greater distress. You may come to believe (as suggested by various books and courses) that you've uncovered all the solutions, but they've failed to yield the desired lasting, profound change. As a result, you might perceive yourself as even more fundamentally flawed than before, as yet another resource has proven ineffective in bringing about the desired transformation.

However, none of that holds true, and it's an incorrect approach regardless. The notion of altering your identity might seem daunting, but it's far less challenging than it initially seems. Confidence and success don't entail departing from your authentic self; instead, they involve returning to the person you've always been. Can you discern the distinction? Can you sense the contrast? One approach suggests that you're inherently flawed, damaged, or broken and must distance yourself from your true self to attain wellness, decency, loveability, and success.

The right way says that you are already all of the things you desire to be.

You've merely overlooked and obscured that remarkable, gifted, and inherently talented individual beneath the burden of misguided teachings, detrimental programming, and stifling societal norms. You see, all these layers of conditioning and instruction shaped your perception of yourself. They didn't define who you truly were; they merely dictated what you were taught to believe about yourself. At a profound level, you instinctively recognized that you were undermining yourself, working against your own interests, and behaving in manners that conflicted with your values and ideals.

Consequently, you developed a dislike for yourself. However, the identity you've struggled to embrace, find solace in, or feel confident about is a product of all this misguided instruction, which isn't a true reflection of who you are.

A significant portion of the guidance presented in this book revolves around precisely this: shedding all the erroneous teachings and societal conditioning that diverted you from your authentic self. By eliminating these obstacles and unlocking the innate success and confidence mindset inherent within you, your life will undergo a profound and enduring transformation. You'll simply be yourself, perhaps for the first time since childhood, and that's precisely why the change will be lasting.

The Essential Mindset Shift for Confidence and Success

There are two basic mindsets: **a fixed mindset and a growth mindset.**

A fixed mindset presupposes that your character, intelligence, talents, and abilities are unchangeable, predetermined traits established at birth. It believes that who you are and what you can achieve are rigid and cannot be significantly altered.

According to this mindset, your life, accomplishments, confidence, and success merely reflect the hand you were dealt at birth. Your achievements serve as validations, assessments, and measurements of these inherent traits.

In contrast, individuals with a growth mindset perceive themselves and the world in a fundamentally different manner. They understand that who they are and what they can achieve are not fixed or static. Instead, they view their character, skills, and abilities as malleable qualities that can be developed and enhanced over time.

For those with a growth mindset, the hand they're dealt serves as a starting point for personal growth and development. They believe that their skills, talents, intelligence, and character can be nurtured through action, practice, and experience. While individuals may differ greatly, everyone has the capacity for change and improvement.

The implications of these contrasting mindsets are profound. Believing that intelligence, personality, and potential are either predetermined or capable of development has far-reaching consequences. Your mindset significantly influences how you navigate life and shapes much of your behavior. Moreover, it profoundly impacts your relationship with success and failure, ultimately shaping your capacity for happiness, confidence, and achievement.

Understanding these mindsets reveals how they influence your actions, decisions, and life paths, shaping your self-perception and impacting your journey towards your desired identity and life goals.

Individuals with fixed mindsets are often preoccupied with proving their abilities, seeking validation from external sources to reinforce their internal beliefs. They may feel compelled to maintain a facade of competence, akin to pretending to hold a winning hand in poker despite doubting its strength beneath the surface. For those with fixed mindsets, failure is dreaded as it threatens to expose their perceived limitations, potentially undermining their sense of self-worth and identity. In contrast, individuals with a growth mindset prioritize learning over seeking approval. They embrace challenges as opportunities for growth and improvement, understanding that setbacks are integral to the learning process.

While both mindsets may encounter failure, their emotional responses differ significantly. Individuals with a growth mindset view failure as a valuable learning experience rather than a reflection of their innate abilities. Rather than concealing their shortcomings, they approach them with curiosity and determination, fostering resilience and adaptive coping strategies.

Embracing a growth mindset fundamentally alters one's outlook on life. Rather than fixating on appearances of intelligence or talent, individuals focus on continuous improvement and development, fostering a mindset conducive to thriving in the face of challenges.

When you adopt a mindset, you step into a different realm. In one realm, characterized by fixed traits, success revolves around demonstrating intelligence or talent, affirming one's abilities. In the alternate realm, defined by evolving attributes, success involves pushing oneself to acquire new knowledge, advancing personal growth.

In one realm, failure entails encountering setbacks like receiving a poor grade, losing a competition, facing dismissal, or experiencing rejection, which suggests a lack of intelligence or talent. Conversely, in the other realm, failure signifies stagnation, a failure to pursue valued objectives, implying an underutilization of one's capabilities.

In one sphere, exerting effort is perceived negatively, akin to failure, indicating a deficit in intelligence or talent. Conversely, in the alternate realm, exerting effort is regarded as the pathway to intelligence and talent.

If you've recognized that you've operated within a fixed mindset thus far, it's a cause for celebration because you've identified a significant barrier to attaining the confidence and success you aspire to achieve. You've pinpointed the obstacle hindering your advancement on your journey.

Realize that you possess the power to choose, a decision you can make at any moment (perhaps even now!) to embrace the mindset shift that dismantles the obstacle before you—the mindset that empowers you to begin unlocking your true potential.

Don't allow your ego to guilt-trip you about the time you believe you've squandered or convince you that change is beyond your reach. Your ego's aim is to maintain your status quo and limit your growth. It inundates you with remorse for the past, undermining you with the false notion that it's too late to alter your course.

Instead, simply acknowledge the truth: you've stumbled upon a solution that empowers you; one that unleashes the talent and greatness you inherently possess, lying dormant until you unleash it.

You can unleash it today

Points for Contemplation

- *Can you start to recognize that you were inherently confident and successful from birth? That confidence and success are your innate state? And that you've merely acquired a set of harmful, constraining, and undermining thought patterns that have hindered this innate confidence and success mindset?*

- *Can you perceive that there's nothing inherently flawed about you, the authentic you, that you're not damaged and don't require repair?*

- Reflect on the idea that the path to confidence and success doesn't involve moving away from your true self, but rather returning to the authentic you—the individual you genuinely are beneath all the negative teaching and misguided beliefs that hinder so many people's potential.

- Do you perceive that lacking this pivotal understanding will ultimately lead books, courses, and therapy to exacerbate your feelings of inadequacy rather than alleviate them? That they will divert you from your innate confidence and success rather than guide you toward it?

- Contemplate whose plan for your life have you been adhering to? Is it a blueprint you crafted for yourself? If given the choice again, would you opt for the same path, or would you opt for something different?

- Reflect on how identity shapes behavior rather than the reverse, and as you recognize the truth about your authentic self, along with the remarkable talents, gifts, and joy you offer to the world, your behavior instinctively begins to evolve accordingly.

- Think about whether you've operated with a fixed mindset without realizing it. Reflect on whether embracing a growth mindset could unlock your extraordinary potential. Contemplate whether you're ready to make that shift today or if delaying serves any purpose.

Instead of passing judgment, simply take a moment to contemplate these questions.

Chapter 2

Mastering the Battle for Mind Control

You possess complete authority over one essential aspect: your thoughts. This divine endowment serves as the solitary mechanism through which you can shape your destiny. Should you neglect to govern your mind, you'll exert control over nothing else.

What if I informed you that there exists a single skill serving as the ultimate key to unlocking all your aspirations? Mastering this skill practically ensures that you'll evolve into the person you aspire to be and lead the life you envision. By acquiring, honing, and ultimately mastering this skill, you'll gain the ability to effortlessly generate success in any realm of your life, dispel any self-imposed limitations, and maintain a composed, confident, and lucid mindset regardless of the circumstances.

To further underscore this point, consider this: What if I informed you that nearly every revered teacher and spiritual guide throughout history has affirmed that this is, in fact, the ultimate secret to life?

For those who aren't inclined towards spirituality, consider this: Tim Ferriss refers to this as the "meta-skill," suggesting that mastering it enables you to enhance all other skills. After conducting over 200 interviews with top performers across various fields, including celebrities, business moguls, athletes, and military leaders, Ferriss concludes that this particular skill distinguishes them from the rest.

Are you curious to find out what it is?

Are you sufficiently intrigued to not only discover it but also to acquire, implement, and refine it until you've honed it to mastery? I trust I have your full attention now, and you grasp the significance of what lies ahead.

The mastery skill is the capacity to govern your mind, directing and concentrating the thoughts you entertain. While it may sound straightforward, fewer than 1 in 100 individuals have truly mastered this art.

The essential inquiry to ponder is this: Do you command your mind, or does your mind command you? Can you soothe your thoughts at will, selecting the ones you wish to entertain? Or does your mind operate on autopilot, inundating you with unproductive, pessimistic notions about potential outcomes and worst-case scenarios?

How frequently does your mind dwell on should-haves, stirring up feelings of regret for past missteps? How often does it divert your attention away from actions that would propel you toward the life you desire, just as you're poised to initiate progress?

Just as you're about to embark on a positive transformation, do you find yourself compelled to check your phone, peruse Instagram, message a friend, or watch YouTube videos?

How many times have your efforts to enact positive changes been thwarted, obstructed, or undermined at every turn? These setbacks occur because you haven't yet mastered the fundamental skill of managing your mind's inner workings.

The Significance of Mind Management

Every action, every emotion, every decision you've ever made traces back to a single origin: your thoughts. Your entire life's trajectory, including your identity, occupation, residence, relationships, financial status, and yes, even your confidence, stems directly from the thoughts circulating in your mind.

Yet, for many, the thoughts they entertain are not consciously chosen; instead, they surrender control to a mind inundated with randomness, chaos, fear, doubt, and self-imposed limitations. Consequently, their achievements and personal growth barely scratch the surface of their innate potential.

Reflect for a moment on your own accomplishments in life; chances are, they're quite substantial.

Despite the lack of control over your mind and the presence of doubts, worries, and fears, you've managed to accomplish so much. Now, envision a scenario where instead of the majority of your thoughts being uncontrollable and negative, they are calm, focused, and directed toward facilitating your progress in life.

Consider the possibilities. You've already achieved remarkable feats against significant odds. Now, imagine the potential when you tilt the odds in your favor. If your predominant thoughts exude confidence, relaxation, happiness, and certainty of success, they become the blueprint for the life you are actively constructing.

Mastering Your Mind

How do you go about mastering control of your mind? The method I'm about to share with you is the most straightforward and effective technique for achieving this.

I learned this technique from my friend and mentor, Garfield Ray, a psychologist. Its effectiveness astonished me during the intense turmoil of a challenging time, keeping me calm, focused, and clear-headed.

Ray initially introduced me to this technique in 2009. Despite my familiarity with Ray and his proven methods, I disregarded his unequivocal advice that this was the most crucial lesson he could impart. It wasn't until six years later, amid the collapse of my life, that I became sufficiently desperate to heed the guidance of a trusted expert and friend.

Ray advised me that the key to mastering my mind was to focus on a single positive thought for 15 uninterrupted seconds—choosing a cherished memory and dwelling on it exclusively for that brief duration.

I attempted this technique for the first time shortly after receiving the news of my father's passing. At that moment, it seemed as though my world was crumbling, and I was besieged by anxiety, tension, fear, pain, and anger. My mind struggled to maintain any thought for even a fraction of a second, darting instead to bleak scenarios and impending hardships faced by my loved ones. The weight of these thoughts bore down on me, leaving me feeling utterly overwhelmed.

However, I recognized that a challenging period lay ahead, one in which difficulties might escalate. I understood that if I didn't break free from this downward spiral, regain mental clarity, and prepare for what lay ahead, the consequences would be dire—not only for the remainder of my life but also for my family.

Thus, I found myself at a point of desperation, willing to take whatever steps necessary.

That day, after concluding my meetings at work, I departed early and embarked on a lengthy walk to clear my mind. I journeyed to one of my cherished spots: a bench on the Southbank overlooking the river. Seated there, I gently closed my eyes and allowed a positive thought to permeate my mind.

The thought that resonated with me was a video of my fiancée, Aeesha. At the time, our relationship was still in its early stages, and we had yet to see each other since we began dating. I had deeply missed her and eagerly anticipated our reunion.

When I called her on a video call and she expressed her excitement about seeing me, it filled me with happiness to know that someone cared for me genuinely. Her radiant face beamed with happiness and anticipation as she exclaimed, "I can't wait to see you," exuding pure joy and excitement.

Even to this day, I struggle to articulate the overwhelming emotions I experienced when I reminisce about that video. The sheer happiness, love, and emotion were indescribable. That was the memory I attempted to concentrate on for just 15 seconds.

However, when I began, I could scarcely maintain that thought for even a single second!

This was one of the happiest and most joyful moments I had ever experienced, yet my mind wouldn't grant me even a moment of peace to relish it. I attempted again, and after several tries, I managed to sustain the positive thought for about two seconds before a flood of negative thoughts invaded.

It dawned on me that I had virtually no command over my own mind. Something beyond my conscious control was dictating its course. It refused to afford me any reprieve to calm down, collect myself, bask in positivity, and momentarily escape the turmoil engulfing my life at that juncture.

Ray had likened the chaotic state of my mind to a "little terrorist," and now it was starkly evident to me. Determined, I persisted, resolved not to vacate that bench until I could sustain my positive thought for a full 15 seconds. It took me a full two hours, but eventually, I achieved it.

That two-hour period was solely dedicated to practicing the technique, with no other distractions. During that time, I progressed from barely managing a second or two to sustaining the positive thought for a full 15 seconds. By the end of those two hours, I felt a sense of calm that had eluded me for months, particularly in the wake of my father's passing. Instead of the usual chaos and negativity, I experienced moments of peace and clarity.

As I walked home, savoring the newfound tranquility, I found that whenever I felt my emotions spiraling out of control or my fears resurfacing, I returned to the 15-second exercise of positive thought. Though I didn't achieve the full duration every time, with each attempt, I improved gradually.

Finally applying the technique that Ray had introduced me to years earlier—albeit one I had previously disregarded—proved to be a turning point. It provided a crucial tool to navigate through my current challenges and pave the way for the life I envisioned. Not only did I feel a greater sense of calm, but, as Ray had predicted, solutions, ideas, insights, and moments of inspiration began to emerge. Problems that once seemed insurmountable became manageable situations, thanks to the clarity and inspiration fostered by a calm mind.

I began to develop the ability to detach and observe the tumult of thoughts racing through my mind—the fears, anxieties, and doomsday scenarios—like a bystander witnessing a spectacle from a distance, rather than being directly embroiled in them. Through continued practice of this technique, I gradually gained mastery over it, until it became a readily accessible tool. Whenever I sensed my mind veering toward chaos, I could employ this technique and swiftly regain control.

This method stands as the paramount factor behind my journey to rebuilding confidence, reclaiming my sense of self, and reconstructing my life. It prevented me from descending into the depths of despair and losing precious years in the process. What once seemed like a journey spanning decades transformed into a mere matter of days, thanks to this technique.

The Process to Reclaiming Your Mind Control

Here's the process:

Recall a memory from your past – the one that brings you the most joy. Choose a memory that, above all others, fills you with happiness and leaves you feeling fantastic whenever you reminisce about it. Select one that resonates with you personally, not one you feel obligated to choose. Opt for a memory that genuinely uplifts your spirits.

What's essential is that you share a profound, positive emotional bond with that memory. It could be a joyful recollection from your childhood, a moment of serene bliss during a vacation, a breathtaking view that left you in awe, a mesmerizing sunrise or sunset, a serene beach, the birth of your child, or a heartwarming interaction with a beloved pet.

Remember, there's no need to justify your selection to anyone else. This is solely for your benefit and personal growth.

Done that ????

Now, recall that memory and gently close your eyes. Allow yourself to fully immerse in it. Absorb every detail.

Experience the emotions you felt when you initially lived that extraordinary moment. Recall the scents, the sounds surrounding you, the sensation of the air against your skin.

Enhance the memory's vividness and depth to your comfort level. Relive that moment; embrace it once more.

Simply dwell in that exquisite, flawless moment. Now, concentrate solely on that thought for 15 seconds. Can you achieve it?

If you attempted this exercise, chances are you struggled to sustain the thought for more than a few seconds at most.

Continue practicing until you can. Don't feel discouraged if progress is gradual. You're acquiring a new skill and overcoming a habit that may have persisted for years. Instead, appreciate and rejoice in taking the initial and vital step toward shaping the life you aspire to.

Be enthusiastic about learning this paramount skill, recognizing that mastering it will open the door to achieving all your desires in life.

Instead of "trying," simply relax and immerse yourself in the thought. Give it a try now.

Did you attempt it, or did you skip past it without giving it a shot?

If you didn't try, reflect on why you chose to bypass this exercise, considering the significance and foundational nature of this skill based on all you've learned.

I can teach you this technique and illustrate the immense costs of not mastering it, as well as the remarkable benefits of becoming the master of your mind. However, ultimately, it's up to you to decide to apply it.

Learning this skill is paramount. It's the initial and most critical step on your journey to becoming the person you aspire to be and living the life you desire. Without reclaiming control of your mind, all your endeavors will ultimately fall short.

If I could travel back in time and offer myself a single piece of advice, it would be to master this skill much earlier.

Now, when you attempt to do this and your mind begins pulling you in various directions, simply detach and observe the chaos unfolding within your mind. Without labeling thoughts as good or bad, as such judgments are unhelpful, observe how your mind flits from one thought to another. Notice that most of these thoughts are fears, doubts, distractions, worries, tasks you've forgotten, or tasks you feel you "should" be doing instead of practicing this exercise.

The Small Troublemaker Inside Your Ear

If you've engaged in that exercise, you've just encountered your ego, the internal saboteur present in all of us.

Whenever you found yourself distracted, fearful, anxious, or doubting yourself during the exercise, it was your ego interfering.

This is the critical voice within your mind that you often mistake for your true self. It inundates you with negative, undermining, limiting, toxic, and harmful thoughts and emotions throughout the day. Every time you internally echo sentiments like "You're not capable," "You can't succeed," "Positive outcomes are beyond your reach," or "You're not deserving of good fortune," it's not genuinely your own voice. It's your ego at work.

If you're feeling uncertain, not living up to your desired lifestyle, and failing to embody the person you aspire to be, this could be the reason. There's an inner saboteur governing your thoughts, engaging in a battle you didn't even realize you were part of.

Pause and consider the implications. If you're anything like I was back then, you're seldom truly in command of your mind. Despite your efforts to enact changes and evolve into your desired self, the true essence of who you are hasn't been leading the way.

And if your thoughts aren't under your control, how can you possibly manage your actions, decisions, and conduct?

I'll delve into various ways your ego undermines your growth, well-being, and aspirations later on. But for now, let's focus on acquainting you with your own ego.

At birth, we enter the world without an ego. This is precisely why we accomplish so much in our early years. From being utterly reliant as infants, by the age of three, we've learned to express joy, move independently, eat, play, and grasp the basics of social interaction. All of this progress occurs because our ego isn't yet obstructing our path.

However, around this age, social conditioning kicks in. As we become more verbal, interactive, and receptive to others' input, we begin to internalize external messages. Because our young minds absorb vast amounts of information without discernment, we start assimilating thought patterns that aren't beneficial to us.

We begin hearing limitations on our capabilities, unlike the unrestricted exploration of our abilities in those initial three years. We encounter expectations about what individuals like us are supposed to be, do, and possess. And notably, we come to understand that affection is conditional.

Consequently, we swiftly adapt to meet the criteria for receiving love. Whether through unintentional absorption or deliberate instruction, we internalize a blueprint of who we ought to be in order to be worthy of love. Prior to age three, the concept of being loved wasn't fully grasped; our actions were simply geared toward fulfilling our needs.

However, around age three, the focus shifts from fulfilling personal desires to conforming to societal "shoulds" in pursuit of love and acceptance—the fundamental desires we all seek. Gradually and often subconsciously, these expectations shape our identity, forming the basis of who we believe ourselves to be.

Before long, these behavioral patterns solidify into the routines guiding your responses to various situations. They morph into your default mode of thinking, so deeply ingrained and normalized that you lose awareness of their presence.

These patterns wield immense power, tethered to the primal need for love and acceptance experienced in childhood—a necessity that feels vital to survival. Over time, interactions with parents, friends, partners, social media, and educators add further layers to this framework, molding you into a fully conditioned adult.

By this stage, the vast majority—about 99%—of individuals find themselves entangled in numerous layers of social conditioning, convoluted thinking, restrictive beliefs, doubts, fears, apprehensions, and a perceived lack of worthiness. Consequently, they become almost entirely disconnected from their authentic selves.

However, not entirely disconnected.

The authentic essence of who you are remains intact, harboring the truth about your capabilities and worthiness. It recognizes that societal conditioning is laden with falsehoods that hinder and burden you. Despite this, it continues to present you with achievable dreams and aspirations. However, your ego, fueled by negativity, opposes these aspirations, triggering a constant internal struggle. This inner conflict, as termed by my colleague Richard Wilkins, manifests as a civil war within your mind. The real you understands that your potential knows no bounds, akin to your state at birth, and recognizes that only distorted thinking obstructs your path to fulfillment. The pain and remorse you experience stem from the deep-seated knowledge of your capability, worthiness, and inherent goodness.

If you were convinced, truly convinced, that your dreams were unattainable, there would be no anguish. The pain arises because deep down, you recognize that these dreams are not only within reach but also readily achievable by your authentic self. However, your ego's primary function is to ensure your safety and maintain a sense of "love" and "acceptance." Therefore, it employs whatever means necessary to halt any progress. Drawing upon your past experiences, it perceives the unknown as a threat. Its paramount concern is to preserve the status quo, believing that familiarity ensures safety. Consequently, every endeavor to improve your circumstances faces immediate and formidable resistance. It inundates you with warnings of dire consequences should you venture beyond your comfort zone, urging you to prioritize worry over embracing the boundless possibilities for your life, reminiscent of the fearless exploration characteristic of your childhood years.

The belief that confidence equates to deceit, resulting in rejection and loss of acceptance, has been ingrained since childhood. You've been inundated with warnings of potential pitfalls should you dare to pursue greatness: launching a business risks financial ruin, approaching an attractive individual may lead to rejection, and the thought of facing such outcomes feels overwhelming. However, the most significant challenge lies in mistaking this critical inner voice for your own. Since early childhood, you've been embroiled in a silent battle for control of your thoughts, unbeknownst to you. Take a moment to pause, as what follows is of utmost importance.

The negative emotions you've experienced about yourself, those moments of feeling inadequate or unworthy, don't truly reflect how you feel about the authentic you.

They're your feelings about your ego.

Your negative emotions are directed towards the internal critic, the voice within your mind that has constantly criticized and belittled you for attempting positive actions or personal growth. This inner critic, your ego, embodies all the negative teachings and influences you've encountered throughout your life. It's understandable that you harbor few positive sentiments towards this aspect of yourself.

In contrast, when you pause and reflect on the authentic you—the one still present within you—you'll find kindness, decency, love, excitement for life, a spirit of adventure, and boundless potential. It's important to approach this process slowly, as your ego may intensify its efforts to undermine these thoughts, urging you to seek distractions like checking social media, listening to music, or attending to chores or emails.

Each of these distractions serves as a ploy by your ego to divert your attention from this pivotal realization because it knows that acknowledging the truth diminishes its hold over you. Unaware of its existence and lacking guidance on how to manage your thoughts, your ego has proliferated and assumed disproportionate control, inundating your mind with convoluted, detrimental, and constraining thoughts.

Upon mastering control of your mind and subduing your ego, the authentic you reclaims authority, empowering you to craft a life aligned with your true desires. Recognizing that your ego does not define you enables you to reestablish a connection with your genuine self—the empowered, authentic version of you—and rediscover your genuine aspirations. This newfound awareness liberates you from the shackles of stifling social conditioning, allowing you to embark on a journey of self-discovery and fulfillment.

Here's the second crucial point I want to emphasize in this section. Take a moment to absorb and reflect on this insight.

Regaining control and allowing the real you to take charge isn't as daunting as it may seem. In fact, you're already proficient at this in various aspects of your life at this very moment. Whether it's excelling in your career, fostering fulfilling relationships, nurturing your children, mastering sports, conquering computer games, showcasing your talents in singing or dancing, or effortlessly making friends, you've already demonstrated mastery in these areas, perhaps without even realizing it. This pattern holds true for anyone who has achieved proficiency in anything—they've discovered ways, whether intentionally or inadvertently, to navigate past the obstacles and barriers erected by their own ego.

They (you) managed to silence the doubts, negative thoughts, limiting beliefs, fears, and expectations, and instead focused on taking the necessary steps to progress.

Do you see? You're already familiar with this mindset in specific areas of your life. Now, the challenge is to extend that approach to all aspects of your life.

The key to overcoming your ego is not to engage in a direct battle with it, but rather to relax and observe its tumultuous behavior. As paradoxical as it may seem, the more you resist and confront your ego, the more power you inadvertently give it.

However, by adopting a relaxed stance and simply witnessing the chaos it generates throughout the day, its influence gradually diminishes. You don't need to forcefully stop it; merely observing its irrationality and assessing whether its thoughts serve your growth or hinder you gradually erodes its authority.

One final note, and I cannot stress this enough: Recognizing your ego and its strategies to keep you stagnant, and mastering control over your thoughts are the fundamental skills you need to develop in order to become the person you aspire to be and craft the life you desire.

Throughout the remainder of this book, I will revisit this point repeatedly. It is only through mastery of your mind that you can harness its full potential in a constructive manner, rather than allowing it to undermine your efforts.

As I reiterate this message, observe how your ego attempts to provoke irritation at the repetition, seeks to distract you, or simply encourages you to avoid practicing the skill because you may believe you already possess it.

Supreme Thought Mastery - Harnessing the "No Mind" Power

Once you've mastered the 15 seconds of positive thought, the next stage, as described by Ray, is what he refers to as "No Mind." This state entails emptying your mind of all thoughts, achieving a state of pure presence, awareness, tranquility, and peace.

In the state of No Mind, all mental chatter subsides and eventually ceases altogether. It's a serene and tranquil experience that envelops me gently. I feel simultaneously connected to the world and detached from it.

To enter this state, I often visualize myself softly descending into a serene, crystal-clear blue sea. As I recline underwater, a sense of silence and peace pervades, and I become completely serene. Despite being aware of my surroundings, I feel isolated from them. Even if turmoil rages above the water's surface, beneath the waves where I reside, there is utter tranquility. Mentally, I surrender to this moment of repose, embracing the sensation of my mind being completely still, open, and serene.

Chapter 3

The Mindset of Highly Successful Individuals

When we look at highly successful individuals, we see something special about them – something that sets them apart. I've always admired their ability to bounce back from setbacks, to see challenges not as roadblocks but as opportunities for growth. They've taught me the importance of resilience – the kind that allows you to come back stronger after every fall.

One thing I've noticed about successful people is their unwavering optimism. Even when faced with tough times, they maintain a positive outlook, believing in their ability to overcome obstacles and reach their goals. It's inspiring to see how their optimism fuels their determination and keeps them moving forward.

Persistence is another quality that stands out. Successful individuals don't give up easily. They have a laser-like focus on their goals and are willing to put in the hard work and effort required to achieve them. I've learned from them that success often comes to those who are willing to stay the course, even when the going gets tough.

Adaptability is another trait that I've admired in successful people. They understand that the world is constantly changing, and they're not afraid to adjust their strategies accordingly. Instead of resisting change, they embrace it, seeing it as an opportunity for growth and innovation.

I've also noticed how successful people are incredibly disciplined. They set clear boundaries for themselves and stick to them, even when it's hard. They understand the importance of delayed gratification and are willing to make sacrifices in the short term for long-term success.

Continuous learning is another area where successful individuals excel. They're always seeking out new knowledge and skills to improve themselves and their abilities. They understand that personal and professional growth is a lifelong journey, and they're committed to self-improvement every step of the way.

Risk-taking is another quality that I've seen in successful people. They're not afraid to step outside of their comfort zone and take calculated risks in pursuit of their goals. They understand that success often requires taking chances and are willing to embrace uncertainty.

Gratitude is another quality that I've noticed in successful individuals. They're grateful for the blessings in their lives and always take the time to acknowledge the contributions of others. They understand that success is not achieved alone and are quick to express their appreciation for the support they receive.

Finally, successful people have a clear vision of what they want to achieve. They have a sense of purpose that guides their actions and decisions, allowing them to stay focused and motivated even in the face of obstacles. Their vision serves as a roadmap for success, helping them navigate the ups and downs of life with confidence and determination.

The mindset traits and habits of highly successful individuals have taught me valuable lessons about resilience, optimism, persistence, adaptability, discipline, continuous learning, risk-taking, gratitude, and vision. By incorporating these qualities into my own life, I hope to unlock my full potential and pursue my goals with confidence and determination.

As I reflect on the mindset of the 1% out of 100% of people that are successful, I realize that there are several key insights we can glean from their approach to life. Adopting and embodying this mindset can help us achieve extraordinary results in our own lives.

First and foremost, the mindset of the 1% is characterized by a relentless commitment to excellence. These individuals strive for greatness in everything they do, refusing to settle for mediocrity. They set high standards for themselves and are willing to put in the work and effort required to surpass them. By adopting this mindset of excellence, we can push ourselves to achieve our full potential and reach heights we never thought possible.

Another key insight from the mindset of the highly successful people is the importance of taking ownership of our actions and decisions. Successful individuals understand that they are in control of their own destiny and refuse to play the role of victim. They take responsibility for their successes and failures alike, viewing every experience as an opportunity for growth and learning. By adopting this mindset of ownership, we can take charge of our lives and create the future we desire.

Furthermore, the mindset they have is characterized by a relentless focus on continuous improvement. Successful individuals are never satisfied with the status quo; they are always looking for ways to grow and evolve. They understand that success is not a destination but a journey, and they are committed to self-improvement every step of the way. By embracing this mindset of growth and learning, we can continuously push ourselves to new heights and achieve extraordinary results.

In addition, the mindset of the highly successful people is characterized by a willingness to embrace discomfort and uncertainty. Successful individuals understand that growth often requires stepping outside of our comfort zones and facing our fears head-on. They are not afraid to take risks or try new things, knowing that failure is simply a stepping stone on the path to success. By adopting this mindset of courage and resilience, we can overcome our fears and limitations and unlock our full potential.

Finally, the mindset is characterized by a deep sense of gratitude and abundance. Successful individuals understand the power of gratitude in attracting more of what they desire into their lives. They are grateful for the opportunities, resources, and support they receive, and they express their appreciation regularly. By adopting this mindset of abundance, we can cultivate a positive outlook on life and attract more success and fulfillment into our lives.

Adopting and embodying the mindset of the successful 1% can help us achieve extraordinary results in our own lives. By committing to excellence, taking ownership of our actions, embracing continuous improvement, facing our fears with courage, and cultivating gratitude and abundance, we can unlock our full potential and create the life of our dreams.

For me, embracing my unique strengths and talents has been a transformative journey that has shaped my personal and professional life in profound ways. I've come to realize that each of us possesses a distinct set of abilities and qualities that make us who we are. Embracing these strengths has allowed me to unlock my full potential and achieve extraordinary results in my endeavors.

One of the most significant benefits of embracing my unique strengths is the sense of authenticity it brings. By recognizing and leveraging my innate talents, I've been able to operate from a place of authenticity, staying true to myself and my values. This authenticity has not only boosted my confidence but has also enabled me to make a genuine impact in the world around me.

Moreover, embracing my unique strengths has ignited a passion and enthusiasm within me that fuels my drive for success. When I engage in activities that align with my strengths, I feel energized and motivated, ready to tackle any challenge that comes my way. This passion has fueled my creativity and innovation, enabling me to find creative solutions to problems and make meaningful contributions in my field.

Additionally, embracing my unique strengths has fostered a deep sense of empowerment and self-acceptance within me. As I've come to embrace and celebrate my strengths, I've developed a greater sense of self-awareness and self-assurance. I've realized that I have valuable gifts to offer the world, and that my unique perspective is worthy of recognition and respect.

Furthermore, embracing my unique strengths has enabled me to cultivate deeper connections and relationships with others. By being authentic and confident in who I am, I've attracted like-minded individuals who appreciate and value me for my genuine self. These strong connections have provided me with a support network that has helped me overcome challenges and achieve my goals.

Finally, embracing my unique strengths has empowered me to make a meaningful impact in my community and society. By leveraging my talents and abilities for the greater good, I've been able to contribute to positive change and transformation. Whether it's through my work, my passions, or my relationships, I've realized that I have the power to make a difference in the world by embracing and sharing my unique strengths.

So, embracing my unique strengths and talents has been a transformative journey that has enriched my life in countless ways. By recognizing and leveraging my innate abilities, I've been able to operate from a place of authenticity, passion, and empowerment. This has enabled me to make a meaningful impact in the world and create a life that is aligned with my true self.

Chapter 4

Releasing Negative Emotional Baggage

When we experience difficult times or traumatic events in our lives, it can really shake our confidence. You know, those moments when it feels like everything is falling apart and we start questioning ourselves and our worth. It's like our self-esteem takes a hit, and we're left feeling vulnerable and unsure of ourselves.

You see, when we go through tough times, it's easy to get stuck in a cycle of negative thinking. We start doubting our abilities and feeling like we're not good enough. It's like our minds get trapped in this loop of self-doubt and insecurity, making it hard to break free.

And it's not just our confidence that takes a hit – our relationships can suffer too. When we've been hurt in the past, it can be really tough to trust others or open up to them. We may even start pushing people away, afraid of getting hurt again.

And let's not forget about how past traumas can hold us back from reaching our goals. When we're carrying around all that baggage from the past, it's like we're weighed down, unable to move forward with confidence. We start second-guessing ourselves and hesitating to take risks, afraid of getting hurt all over again.

But you know what? Healing is possible. It may not be easy, but it's possible. One way to start healing is by talking to someone – a therapist, a counselor, a trusted friend. Just having someone to listen can make a world of difference.

And taking care of ourselves is important too. Engaging in activities that make us feel good, like exercising or meditating, can help us manage stress and build resilience. And surrounding ourselves with supportive people who lift us up can make a big difference too.

But perhaps the most important thing we can do is show ourselves some compassion. It's easy to be hard on ourselves, but we need to remember that we're only human. We've been through a lot, and we deserve to be kind to ourselves as we heal and grow.

So, yes, past traumas and negative experiences can really impact our confidence. But with time, patience, and a little bit of self-love, we can overcome them and build a brighter, more empowered future for ourselves.

Releasing emotional baggage and building emotional resilience are such crucial parts of our journey toward healing and growth. You know, when we carry around all those unresolved emotions from the past, it's like we're dragging around a heavy weight that holds us back from fully living our lives.

But there are some techniques that can really help us lighten that load and build up our inner strength:

First off, there's mindfulness. It's all about tuning into our thoughts and feelings without judging them. Taking a few moments to breathe deeply and check in with ourselves can really help us understand where our emotional baggage is coming from.

And then there's journaling. It's amazing how putting pen to paper and letting our thoughts flow can help us make sense of our emotions. Writing it all down can give us clarity and insight into what's been weighing us down.

Of course, seeking support from others is so important too. Whether it's talking to a therapist, joining a support group, or just confiding in a trusted friend, having someone to lean on can make a world of difference. Knowing that we're not alone in our struggles can be incredibly comforting.

And let's not forget about self-care. Taking time to do things that nourish our body, mind, and soul – like going for a walk in nature, practicing yoga, or indulging in a hobby we love – can help us recharge and build up our resilience.

Changing our perspective can also be really powerful. Sometimes, our emotional baggage is tied to negative beliefs we have about ourselves or the world around us. By challenging those beliefs and choosing to see things in a more positive light, we can free ourselves from the weight of the past.

And last but not least, forgiveness. It's not always easy, but letting go of resentment and bitterness – both toward ourselves and others – can be incredibly liberating. Forgiveness isn't about excusing someone's behavior; it's about releasing ourselves from the grip of anger and pain so we can move forward with our lives.

So, yeah, releasing emotional baggage and building emotional resilience may not happen overnight, but with patience, compassion, and a little bit of effort, we can lighten that load and embrace life with open arms.

Chapter 5

Healing from the Cancer of Pleasing People

When we constantly seek to please others, it can actually do more harm than good. You know, always putting others' needs and desires ahead of our own can leave us feeling drained and unfulfilled. It's like we're constantly running on empty, trying to keep everyone happy while ignoring our own needs in the process.

One of the biggest problems with people-pleasing is that we tend to sacrifice our own values and boundaries in the name of making others happy. We might say yes to things we don't really want to do or agree with opinions that don't align with our own, just to avoid rocking the boat. But in the end, we end up betraying ourselves and our own sense of integrity.

And let's talk about boundaries – or rather, the lack thereof. When we're constantly trying to please others, we often struggle to assert ourselves and set healthy boundaries in our relationships. We might let people walk all over us or avoid speaking up for fear of upsetting others. But by neglecting our own boundaries, we're essentially giving others permission to disregard them too.

On top of that, people-pleasing can really take a toll on our confidence. When we're constantly seeking validation from others, our self-worth becomes dependent on their approval. And when we don't meet their expectations, we end up feeling inadequate and insecure. It's like our confidence takes a hit every time we prioritize someone else's happiness over our own.

But perhaps the most damaging aspect of people-pleasing is the toll it takes on our authenticity. When we're so focused on pleasing others, we lose sight of who we really are and what we truly want. We end up wearing a mask, pretending to be someone we're not just to fit in or avoid conflict. And in the end, we end up feeling disconnected from ourselves and others.

So yeah, people-pleasing might seem like the polite and selfless thing to do, but in reality, it can do more harm than good. It's important to recognize the pitfalls of people-pleasing and prioritize our own needs and boundaries. By asserting ourselves, setting healthy boundaries, and staying true to ourselves, we can cultivate a greater sense of confidence, authenticity, and fulfillment in our lives.

Setting healthy boundaries and prioritizing self-care are vital for breaking free from the exhausting cycle of people-pleasing and reclaiming our confidence and well-being. One thing I've learned is that communication is key. Learning to speak up for ourselves and express our needs and limits in a clear and respectful manner can make a huge difference. It's about finding that balance between being assertive and considerate of others' feelings.

Another important lesson I've learned is the power of saying no. It's okay to decline requests or invitations that don't align with our priorities or values. Saying no doesn't make us selfish; it's about protecting our time and energy for the things that truly matter to us.

Self-awareness is also crucial in setting healthy boundaries. Taking the time to check in with ourselves and assess how we're feeling physically, mentally, and emotionally can help us recognize when our boundaries are being crossed. This awareness allows us to take proactive steps to address the situation before it escalates.

And let's not forget the importance of seeking support from others. Having someone to confide in and bounce ideas off of can provide valuable perspective and validation. Whether it's a friend, family member, or therapist, having a supportive network can make all the difference in setting and maintaining healthy boundaries.

As for self-care, it's something I've come to realize is non-negotiable. Making time for activities that nourish our body, mind, and soul is essential for maintaining our overall well-being. Whether it's going for a walk in nature, practicing yoga, or indulging in a favorite hobby, self-care allows us to recharge our batteries and approach life with renewed energy and resilience.

Chapter 6

How to Eliminate Fear, Worry and Doubt

Fear, worry, and doubt are emotions that we all experience at some point in our lives, and they can be pretty tough to deal with. But have you ever stopped to think about where these feelings come from? Well, it turns out there are a few root causes that contribute to them.

One big one is past experiences. You know, when something scary or traumatic happens to us, it can leave a lasting impression. Those experiences can stick with us, creating fears and worries that linger long after the event is over. For example, if we've been in a car accident, we might develop a fear of driving or constantly worry about being in another accident.

Then there are learned behaviors and beliefs. From the time we're little, we're influenced by the people and world around us. If we grow up in an environment where failure is frowned upon, we might start doubting our abilities and worrying about not measuring up. And let's not forget about societal pressures – they can play a big role too. Constant exposure to negative news stories or unrealistic standards of success can fuel our fears and insecurities.

On top of that, there are psychological factors at play too. Things like low self-esteem or negative thinking patterns can make us more prone to fear, worry, and doubt. If we don't feel good about ourselves or we're always expecting the worst, it's no wonder we end up feeling scared and anxious.

And then there are environmental factors. When life gets stressful or uncertain, it's natural to feel afraid and worried. Major life changes, like moving to a new place or starting a new job, can also trigger feelings of doubt and insecurity as we navigate unfamiliar territory.

But here's the thing – understanding where these feelings come from is the first step to overcoming them. By recognizing the root causes of our fears, worries, and doubts, we can start to challenge them and take back control of our lives. It's not always easy, but with self-awareness, support from others, and a little bit of courage, we can learn to face our fears head-on and live more fully and authentically.

Reframing negative thoughts and beliefs is like giving ourselves a mental makeover – it's all about shifting our perspective to see things in a more positive light. Here are some ways to do it:

First off, let's start by paying attention to our thoughts. When we catch ourselves thinking negatively, it's important to pause and ask ourselves if those thoughts are really true. Are we just jumping to conclusions, or is there evidence to support what we're thinking? By questioning our negative thoughts, we can start to challenge them and see things more realistically.

Next, let's work on replacing those negative thoughts with more positive ones. It's all about finding a more balanced perspective. So instead of thinking, "I'll never be good enough," we can reframe it as, "I may not be perfect, but I'm capable and worthy of success." It's amazing how just changing the way we think can change how we feel.

And let's not forget about being kind to ourselves. We're often our own worst critics, but it's important to remember that we're only human. It's okay to make mistakes and have flaws – that's what makes us unique. So let's practice self-compassion and treat ourselves with the same kindness and understanding that we would a good friend.

Another thing we can do is focus on what we're grateful for. It's easy to get caught up in what's going wrong, but taking time to appreciate the things that are going right can really shift our perspective. Whether it's a beautiful sunset or a kind gesture from a friend, there's always something to be grateful for.

And last but not least, let's surround ourselves with positivity. Whether it's spending time with supportive friends and family, engaging in activities that bring us joy, or limiting our exposure to negative influences like the news or social media, surrounding ourselves with positivity can really lift our spirits and help us see the brighter side of life.

So there you have it – reframing negative thoughts and beliefs is all about shifting our perspective and embracing a more positive outlook on life. It may take some practice, but with patience and persistence, we can train our minds to see the good in every situation and live with more courage, optimism, and resilience.

Also let's talk about Negative self-talk and limiting beliefs. These can really take a toll on our confidence and happiness. You know, when we're constantly criticizing ourselves or telling ourselves that we're not good enough, it's like we're putting up roadblocks to our own success and fulfillment.

But the good news is, there are ways to break free from this cycle of negativity and replace it with positivity and self-empowerment. One thing we can do is start paying attention to our thoughts. When we catch ourselves thinking negatively, we can challenge those thoughts and replace them with more positive ones. It's all about consciously shifting our mindset and choosing to focus on the good instead of dwelling on the bad.

Another thing we can do is question our limiting beliefs. You know, those thoughts that tell us we're not capable or worthy of success? Well, they're just that – beliefs, not facts. By questioning the validity of these beliefs and looking for evidence to the contrary, we can start to chip away at them and replace them with more empowering perspectives.

And let's not forget about being kind to ourselves. It's easy to be our own worst critic, but we deserve better than that. Instead of beating ourselves up for our perceived shortcomings, let's treat ourselves with kindness and compassion. We're only human, after all, and we're doing the best we can.

Surrounding ourselves with positivity can also make a big difference. Whether it's spending time with supportive friends and family, seeking out uplifting content, or engaging in activities that bring us joy, surrounding ourselves with positivity can help reinforce our efforts to cultivate a more positive mindset.

And finally, there's no shame in seeking professional support if we need it. Therapists and counselors are trained to help us challenge negative thought patterns, build confidence, and cultivate self-compassion. Sometimes, a little extra support and guidance can make all the difference in overcoming self-doubt and embracing our true potential.

So, yes, negative self-talk and limiting beliefs can be tough to overcome, but with awareness, perseverance, and a little help from others, we can replace them with positivity and self-empowerment. And when we do, we'll be amazed at how much happier and more confident we feel.

Chapter 7

Unleashing Your Natural Abundance

The abundance mindset is like having a pair of glasses that helps us see the world in a whole new light. It's all about believing that there's more than enough success, opportunities, and blessings to go around for everyone. Instead of seeing life as a competition where there's only so much to go around, it's about recognizing the limitless possibilities and resources available to us.

One of the coolest things about the abundance mindset is how it's connected to the idea of the law of attraction. You know, the idea that what we focus on, we attract into our lives? Well, when we focus on abundance and success, we tend to attract more of it. It's like the universe responds to our positive energy and sends even more good stuff our way.

But it's not just about material wealth – it's about appreciating all the abundance that surrounds us. From the love of family and friends to the beauty of nature to the opportunities for growth and learning, there's so much to be grateful for. And when we focus on all the good things in our lives, we open ourselves up to even more blessings and opportunities.

Another cool thing about the abundance mindset is how it helps us approach challenges and setbacks. Instead of seeing obstacles as roadblocks, we see them as opportunities for growth and learning. It's like we approach life with a sense of curiosity and resilience, knowing that every challenge is just another chance to grow stronger and wiser.

And let's not forget about taking action. The abundance mindset isn't just about sitting back and waiting for good things to happen – it's about going out there and making them happen. Whether it's pursuing our dreams, taking calculated risks, or seizing opportunities when they arise, it's all about being proactive and taking charge of our lives.

But perhaps the coolest thing about the abundance mindset is how it inspires generosity and kindness. Instead of hoarding our blessings out of fear of scarcity, we're more inclined to share them with others. We understand that by giving freely and supporting others, we create a ripple effect of abundance that benefits everyone.

The abundance mindset is pretty awesome. It's about seeing the world as a place of endless possibilities and opportunities, and living with gratitude, optimism, and generosity. And when we embrace the abundance mindset, we open ourselves up to a life filled with purpose, passion, and fulfillment.

Cultivating gratitude and abundance consciousness is all about shifting our perspective and training our minds to focus on the positive. Here are some simple exercises to help you get started:

- **1. Gratitude journaling:** Take a few minutes each day to write down three things you're grateful for. It could be anything – from the people in your life to the little moments of joy you experience each day. Writing down what you're grateful for helps you appreciate the abundance that already exists in your life.

- **2. Visualization:** Set aside some time each day to visualize yourself living a life of abundance and success. Close your eyes and imagine yourself achieving your goals, surrounded by love, happiness, and prosperity. Visualizing success helps you believe in the abundance that's possible for you.

- **3. Affirmations:** Repeat positive affirmations to yourself throughout the day to reinforce your abundance mindset. Affirmations are simple statements like "I am worthy of abundance" or "I attract success into my life." Saying these affirmations helps you shift your mindset from scarcity to abundance.

- **4. Acts of kindness:** Practice random acts of kindness towards others to cultivate a sense of abundance and generosity. It could be as simple as holding the door open for someone or complimenting a stranger. Acts of kindness remind you of the abundance of love and compassion in the world.

- **5. Abundance meditation:** Spend a few minutes each day meditating on abundance and gratitude. Find a quiet space, close your eyes, and focus on your breath. With each inhale, imagine yourself breathing in abundance and gratitude. With each exhale, release any feelings of scarcity or lack.

- **6. Gratitude walks:** Take a walk outside and use the time to reflect on everything you're grateful for. Notice the beauty of nature around you – the colors, sounds, and smells. Allow yourself to feel a sense of awe and appreciation for the abundance of life.

- **7. Create an abundance vision board:** Gather images, quotes, and affirmations that represent the abundance you want to manifest in your life and create a vision board. Display your vision board somewhere you'll see it every day as a reminder of your abundance goals and intentions.

Cultivating gratitude and abundance consciousness is a practice that takes time and effort. But the more you focus on gratitude and abundance, the more abundance you'll attract into your life. So embrace these exercises with an open heart and watch as your life transforms with abundance and blessings.

Chapter 8

The Strength of Perspectives

Perspective is like the lens through which we view the world, and it has a huge impact on our confidence and success. Let's break it down:

First off, perspective influences how we see ourselves. If we have a positive perspective, we're more likely to believe in ourselves and our abilities. We see challenges as opportunities and setbacks as chances to learn and grow. On the flip side, if our perspective is negative, we may doubt ourselves and our worth. We might let setbacks knock us down, seeing them as proof that we're not good enough. This difference in perspective can determine whether we go after our goals with confidence or hold ourselves back out of fear.

Moreover, perspective shapes how we handle setbacks and failures. If we have a growth-oriented perspective, we see setbacks as temporary roadblocks, not permanent barriers. We're resilient and bounce back from failure with renewed determination. But if our perspective is fixed, we might see failure as a sign that we're not cut out for success. We may give up easily, believing that we'll never be able to overcome our challenges.

Furthermore, perspective affects how we approach change and challenges. If we have an open-minded perspective, we see change as a natural part of life and challenges as opportunities for growth. We're adaptable and embrace new experiences with enthusiasm. But if our perspective is closed-minded, we may resist change, clinging to what's familiar out of fear of the unknown. This resistance can hold us back from seizing new opportunities and reaching our full potential.

Additionally, perspective shapes our relationships with others. If we have an empathetic and open-minded perspective, we're more likely to connect with people from different backgrounds and viewpoints. We value diversity and seek to understand others' perspectives. This ability to empathize and collaborate is essential for success in both personal and professional relationships. However, if our perspective is closed-off or judgmental, we may struggle to connect with others and may find ourselves at odds with those around us.

Perspective plays a crucial role in shaping our confidence and success in life. By cultivating a positive and growth-oriented perspective, we can overcome challenges with resilience, embrace change with enthusiasm, and build positive relationships with others. It's all about seeing the world through a lens of possibility and opportunity, rather than limitation and fear.

Shifting perspectives is a powerful tool for overcoming challenges and seizing opportunities in life. Here are some techniques to help you cultivate a more positive and open-minded outlook:

Firstly, practice mindfulness and self-awareness. Take time each day to reflect on your thoughts, emotions, and reactions to different situations. Notice when you're feeling stuck or resistant to change, and challenge yourself to consider alternative perspectives. By becoming more aware of your own thought patterns, you can begin to identify and shift limiting beliefs that may be holding you back.

Moreover, seek out new experiences and viewpoints. Step outside of your comfort zone and expose yourself to diverse perspectives and ideas. This could involve reading books, watching documentaries, or attending workshops and events that challenge your assumptions and broaden your horizons. Engaging with different perspectives can help you see the world in a new light and open yourself up to new possibilities.

Additionally, practice reframing negative thoughts and beliefs. When faced with a challenge or setback, try to see it from a different angle. Instead of viewing it as a roadblock, ask yourself what opportunities or lessons it might present. Look for silver linings and positive aspects in every situation, no matter how challenging it may seem. By reframing your perspective, you can transform obstacles into opportunities for growth and learning.

Furthermore, cultivate gratitude and appreciation for what you have. Take time each day to focus on the things you're grateful for, whether it's your health, relationships, or simple pleasures like a beautiful sunset. Cultivating a mindset of gratitude can help you shift your perspective from scarcity to abundance, allowing you to see opportunities where you once saw only challenges.

Moreover, surround yourself with positive influences and supportive people. Spend time with friends and family who uplift and inspire you, and seek out mentors or role models who embody the mindset and values you aspire to. Surrounding yourself with positivity can help reinforce your efforts to shift your perspective and overcome challenges with confidence and resilience.

Lastly, practice visualization and goal-setting. Take time to visualize your goals and dreams as if they've already come true. Imagine yourself overcoming obstacles, seizing opportunities, and achieving success. By visualizing your desired outcomes, you can create a mental roadmap for how to get there and cultivate the mindset and motivation to make it happen.

Shifting perspectives is a powerful tool for overcoming challenges and seizing opportunities in life. By practicing mindfulness, seeking out new experiences, reframing negative thoughts, cultivating gratitude, surrounding yourself with positivity, and visualizing your goals, you can cultivate a more positive, open-minded outlook and approach life with confidence and resilience.

Conclusion

In conclusion, "The Unshakeable Confidence: Strategies to Build Unstoppable Confidence in Order to Achieve Goals and Live a Fulfilling Life" has been a comprehensive guide on how to harness the power of our minds to cultivate unshakeable confidence and achieve our deepest aspirations. Throughout this journey, we've delved into the intricacies of controlling our minds, understanding that our thoughts have the profound ability to shape our reality.

At the heart of this book lies the recognition that confidence is not a fixed trait, but a skill that can be developed and nurtured over time. By adopting the strategies and principles outlined within these chapters, we have uncovered the keys to cultivating unshakeable confidence – confidence that empowers us to overcome obstacles, pursue our goals, and live life on our own terms.

One of the fundamental lessons we've learned is the importance of mindset in shaping our reality. Our beliefs, attitudes, and perceptions play a crucial role in determining our level of confidence and our ability to achieve success. By shifting our perspective from one of scarcity and limitation to one of abundance and possibility, we open ourselves up to a world of opportunities and potential.

Moreover, we've discovered that confidence is not just about how we feel about ourselves, but how we navigate the challenges and uncertainties of life. Through the strategies outlined in this book, we've learned to embrace failure as a stepping stone to success, to view setbacks as opportunities for growth, and to approach challenges with resilience and determination.

Furthermore, we've explored the role of self-awareness and self-compassion in cultivating confidence. By becoming more attuned to our thoughts, emotions, and behaviors, we gain insight into the underlying beliefs and patterns that may be holding us back. Through practices such as mindfulness, journaling, and reflection, we've learned to challenge negative self-talk, cultivate a sense of self-worth, and nurture a deep sense of compassion for ourselves and others.

Additionally, we've delved into the power of visualization and goal-setting in manifesting our desires. By envisioning our goals with clarity and intention, we set in motion a series of actions and behaviors that align us with our highest aspirations. Through the practice of visualization, we tap into the creative power of our minds to bring our dreams to life and to propel us towards our desired outcomes.

Furthermore, we've explored the importance of taking proactive steps towards building confidence in our daily lives. Whether it's setting small, achievable goals, stepping outside of our comfort zones, or surrounding ourselves with positive influences, we've learned that confidence is not just a state of mind, but a way of being in the world.

Moreover, we've discovered that confidence is not a solo endeavor, but a journey that is enriched by the support and encouragement of others. Through the power of connection and community, we've found strength in sharing our experiences, seeking guidance from mentors and role models, and offering support to those on a similar path.

In essence, "The Unshakeable Confidence" is more than just a book – it's a call to action, a roadmap to personal transformation, and a testament to the boundless potential that lies within each of us. As we close the final chapter and embark on the next stage of our journey, let us carry with us the lessons learned, the insights gained, and the wisdom shared. Let us embody the principles of confidence, resilience, and empowerment in every aspect of our lives, and let us continue to strive towards a future filled with passion, purpose, and possibility.

Leaving a Review

Dear Reader,

I trust this message reaches you in good spirits. I want to convey my heartfelt gratitude for delving into the contents of this book. Our shared exploration has been incredibly meaningful, and I sincerely hope you found the book enlightening and valuable.

As the author, your perspective holds significant value for me. I would greatly appreciate it if you could take a moment to share your thoughts and impressions by leaving a review wherever you obtained the book. Your feedback not only offers me valuable insights but also helps other readers in discovering and assessing the book's suitability to their interests. Whether you opt for a brief comment or a more elaborate review, your honest feedback is deeply appreciated.

Thank you once more for being a vital participant in this literary journey. I look forward eagerly to hearing your thoughts and wish to express my sincere appreciation for your time and thoughtfulness.

Warm regards,

Ruben B. Campbell

www.ingramcontent.com/pod-product-compliance
Lightning Source LLC
Chambersburg PA
CBHW070425290526
45791CB00005B/1834